AF480041

She likes to wear her polka dot dress and
carry her duffle bag, filled with her
colored pencils and drawing paper,
everywhere she goes. She loves to
create, paint, and imagine.

She loves reading and spending time in
nature, playing with her cat and watching
the beautiful creatures around her.

She can watch for hours as a caterpillar
transforms into a butterfly. Her goal is
to fit in, to feel like she belongs.

Her biggest fear is that she does not fit;
and that everyone will make fun of her.

This is a magical journey to help her find
the happy moments of joy and bliss; to
offer answers to her inner uncertainties
and doubts so that she can blossom into
the beautiful girl she is from within.

In her first picture book, author and illustrator, Tammy Machmali encapsulates the internal emotions felt by many girls. In the book, Tammy Machmali's intention is to elevate and encourage the girl who is feeling uncertainties and doubts. This book is filled with affirmations and positive words, so that girls can be present to experience moments of joy and bliss.

**To Hertzel, Hila, Liad, and Baba
Arastoo my grandfather**

All rights reserved. No part of this book may be reproduced, transmitted, or stored in an information retrieval system in any form or by any means, electronics, or mechanical, including photocopying, taping, and recording, without prior written permission from the author.

Beautiful Girl

Affirmations for Little Queens

by Tammy Machmali

Beautiful girl,

every once in while,
a day comes along
when you simply can't smile.

The world may feel hard
or frustrating at times,
You may find you're not quickest
to finish the rhymes.

You'll feel out of sorts,
But you won't know just why
Things may not feel right
And you just want to cry.

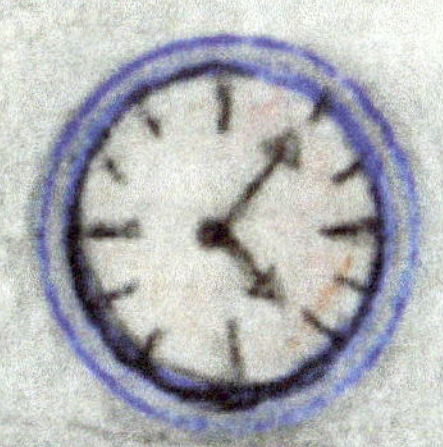

cos(-x) = cos(x)
90°
l x w x h = Area
∛-8 = -∛8 = -2
y = kx² k>0
X² + (y-³√x²)² = 1
Δm = ΔEO / O²
Δf = ∇²f = ∇·∇f
π ≈ 3.1419
y = k/x k<0
V = ⅓πr²h
MV / √(1-v²/c²)
a/b
Sinθ/cosθ
√x(x-a)(x-6)
y
B
C
d
a
A D c
Σ j = j³
(a+b)² = a² + 2ab + b²
1 2 3 4
5 6 7 8
9 10 11 12
13 14 15 16
17 18 19 20

Beautiful Girl!

Feelings come and they go.
Emotions will make you swing high and swing low.
When you're angry, or lonely,
you may want to bawl.

When you feel frustrated
You'll stomp down the hall.
But wait, take a minute—,
Examine your soul.
Assess what you're feeling
That should be your goal.

Beautiful Girl!

Some days, you may feel blue
You may not be sure about
what you should do.

You may feel like you
want to just run off and hide;
to be on your own
with no one by your side,
To pause and rewind,
to unplug and slow down,
Until you can straighten
That sad little frown.

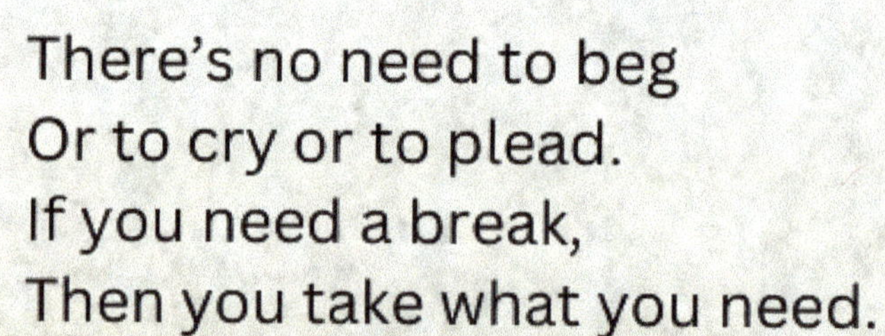

There's no need to beg
Or to cry or to plead.
If you need a break,
Then you take what you need.

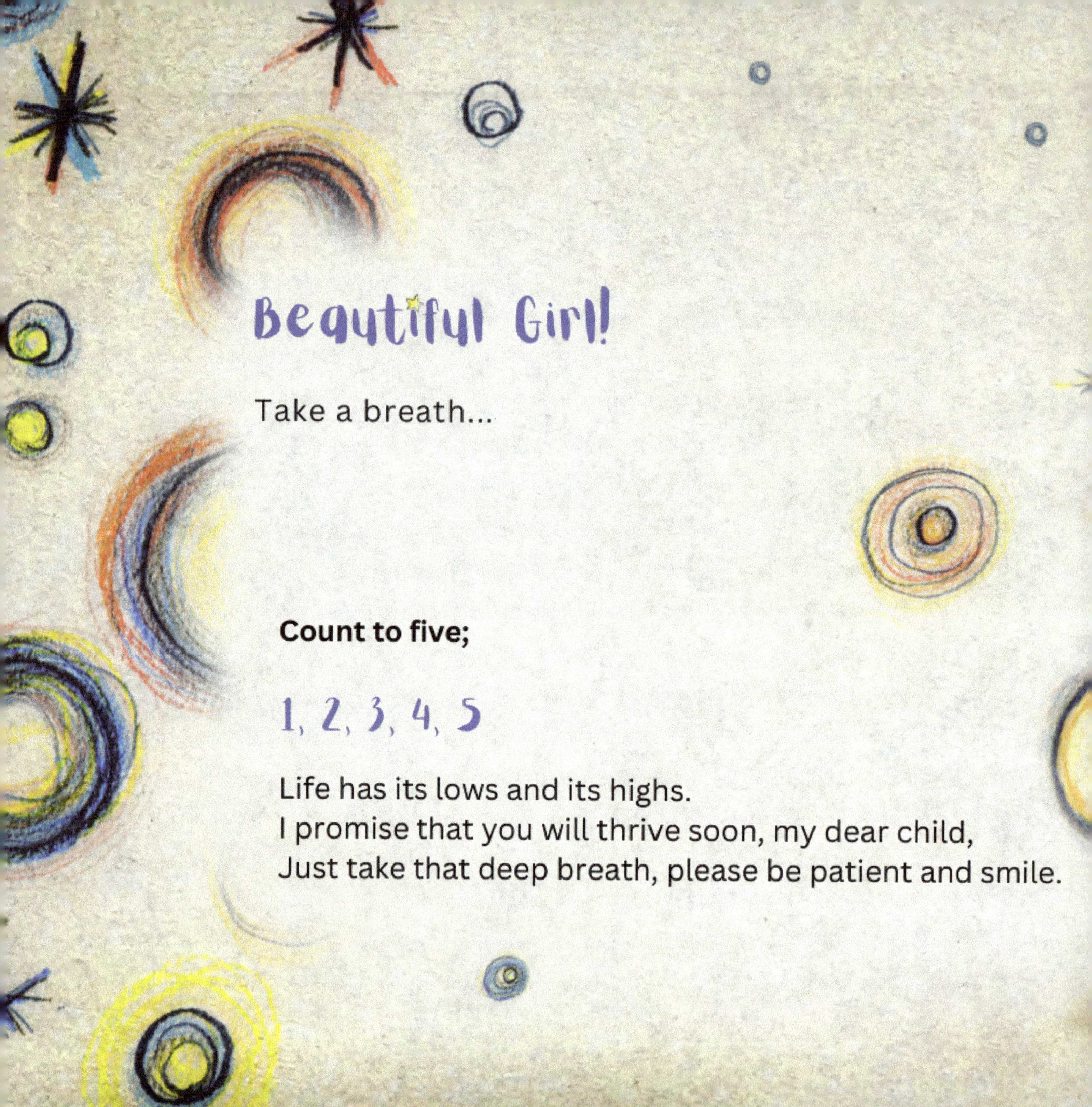

Beautiful Girl!

Take a breath...

Count to five;

1, 2, 3, 4, 5

Life has its lows and its highs.
I promise that you will thrive soon, my dear child,
Just take that deep breath, please be patient and smile.

1
2
3
4
5

Beautiful Girl!

Sometimes, you'll **feel too tall—;**
too short, or too big, or you may feel too small.

It may be that you will not feel like you are
the most beautiful or the smartest by far.
You may feel too awkward, you may feel too shy,
perhaps you will feel like you need a good cry.

Know that you ARE perfectly ENOUGH no matter what.

Beautiful Girl!

Spending time walking in through trees
The world all around you
Has so much to see.
Know that each tree,
And each grass blade and every flower,
Holds its own art and
its own healing power.

LISTEN!

Yes, please listen.
to your perfect art:
The thoughts deep inside you
And what's in your heart.

The voice deep within you is your gentle guide,
There are no wrong feelings,
there is no need to hide.
Say what you are thinking,
But always be kind;
Show love and respect
To the people you find.

Beautiful Girl!

Let us just pause right there...
When you feel unhappy or
Life seems unfair.

PLEASE, DON'T GIVE UP

Just because you are scared.
Your feelings are something that
Ought to be shared.
Even on days when you don't feel just right,
In someone's heart,
You are still loved and are bright.

Beautiful Girl!

Please, remember there's room
For all of the **LIGHT** that's inside you to **BLOOM**.
To be bold and fast,
to be loud and be smart.

It's your birthright to be loved for what's in your heart,
and supported no matter what.
So go out and let the whole world see your light

Spread it around and remember, SHINE bright.

Beautiful Girl!

Gratitude takes you far.
Remember the best things
in life always are
free and of no charge;
the people you love,
Like good laughs and kisses
And lots of big hugs.

Ask your mom for a hug,
and hold on for a while!
Let her bug you out with her too-big smile.

Beautiful Girl!

This is the perfect time.
This is your moment to be in your prime.
To dream and create
And of course to explore.

To enjoy, have fun and so, so much more!
to run,
to hug,
to snuggle,
to be and just Love!

Enjoy the love coming at you from above.
Here and right now, oh my dear,

You're **A STAR**,

Know you are perfect the way that you are,
And this is your time!

A NOTE FROM TAMMY MACHMALI

For my amazing daughters Hila and Liad.
May you always hear and follow your inner guidance
and your callings.

And for you, the reader, who inspired me to write this
book. In this book you will find affirmations, kind
words, and encouragement that I want to say to girls
and women all over the world. This book is for all those
who feel deeply, and are looking for meaning.

May this book motivate you to awaken the power of
your own abilities so that you can use it in your own
life and share it with others.